"Why read yet another Advent devotional? *Christmas with Luke*, by Pastor Scott Wade, gives readers new opportunities to escape their busy lives to quickly and quietly focus on Jesus' love, provision, and protection for all people. Pastor Wade provides favorable conditions for individual thought, small-group conversation, and family experiences as he reminds us to concentrate on Jesus during the Advent season. Offering various tools to promote thought and conversation, the author sharpens our focus on scripture during this season. Join Pastor Wade and the apostle Luke and encounter Christ actively this Christmas."

Dr. Patty Hambrick
Super Life/Super Bus Neighborhood
Mentoring Coordinator
Faculty member emerita (retired),
former director of academic technology
and academic grants, and professor
of education, Charleston Southern University
Charleston, South Carolina

"For busy families who are wanting to instill the true meaning of Christmas to their children, this is a great book that supports the story of Jesus' birth. It includes activities that will help young kids understand what Christmas is truly about. Parents will have all they need at their fingertips to support the biblical story of Jesus' birth."

Tonya Swisshelm
Mother and public school teacher

christmas
with luke

SCOTT WADE
with MATT & FAY WAGNER

dustjacket

ISBN: 978-1-947671-66-9

Published by Dust Jacket Press
Christmas with Luke/Scott Wade with Matt and Fay Wagner

Dust Jacket Press
P.O. Box 721243
Oklahoma City, OK 73172
www.dustjacket.com

Scripture quotations not otherwise designated are from The Holy Bible, English Standard Version. ESV® Text Edition: 2016. Copyright © 2001 by Crossway Bibles, a publishing ministry of Good News Publishers.

Permission to quote from the following additional copyrighted version of the Bible is acknowledged with appreciation:

The Holy Bible, New International Version®, NIV® Copyright ©1973, 1978, 1984, 2011 by Biblica, Inc.® Used by permission. All rights reserved worldwide.

Dust Jacket logos are registered trademarks of Dust Jacket Press, Inc.

Cover & interior design: D. E. West / ZAQ Designs & Dust Jacket Creative Services

Printed in the United States of America

www.dustjacket.com

DEDICATION

This book is dedicated to my friend and mentee, Kenny McQuitty. Kenny has always been able to "tie a ribbon" on things I've initiated. From sermons to seminars, from teaching to training, from rites to writing, Kenny just seems to know what I'm thinking—and how to get us out of the mess I've gotten us into! Kenny, thanks for helping me get this project from "concept to cover."

CONTENTS

FOREWORD

There are many Christmas devotionals out there. Very few of them go to the effort to include the family as a whole, something about which I am quite passionate! Without holistic, integrated, family-centered discipleship we are left all too often with a critical hole in spiritual formation. Scott Wade helps bring us back onto the journey toward rectifying this lapse. This devotional engages all age groups in the family. It promotes discussion among them by keeping them all on the same topic each day. This is a great resource to help bring families back together under a common, formational spiritual umbrella. If you desire your family to grow together toward each other and God, then this is a great way spend your Christmas season!

God's best to you!

Dave Foshee
Lead Pastor
Engage Church
Shawnee, Kansas

ACKNOWLEDGMENTS

Special thanks to Matt and Fay Wagner—friends of God and friends of mine—for their excellent discussion questions and activities geared toward children and families.

Thank you also to Lana, my wife, for her encouragement as I wrote and for providing gentle suggestions as she proofread the manuscript.

To Adam Toler and the staff at Dust Jacket—thanks for your wonderful leadership and expert advice in getting this project from plan to page.

I'm grateful for the work of my editor, Jonathan Wright, who made sure that the mess I had made got all cleaned up and presentable!

INTRODUCTION

THAT YOU MAY HAVE CERTAINTY

Inasmuch as many have undertaken to compile a narrative of the things that have been accomplished among us, just as those who from the beginning were eyewitnesses and ministers of the word have delivered them to us, it seemed good to me also, having followed all things closely for some time past, to write an orderly account for you, most excellent Theophilus, that you may have certainty concerning the things you have been taught. (Luke 1:1–4)

Luke, a follower of God, wrote to Theophilus, a friend of God, "You may have certainty concerning the things you have been taught."

Like Theophilus, are you a friend of God? And would you like to have a little more certainty in your life? Is that desire for certainty even more acute in this time when the very "reason for the season" has come under attack?

Come journey with Luke, a medical doctor and missionary, from Nazareth to Bethlehem, from Jerusalem to Judea, from Galilee to Golgotha. As you do so, you will walk in the footsteps of Jesus Christ, the Son of God. Come make the journey to *Christmas with Luke*.

Don't make this journey alone. Invite someone to join you, that that person too "may have certainty concerning the things [he or she has] been taught."

ADVENT:
The Arrival of a Notable Person or Thing

*A*dvent is an anglicized form of the Latin *adventus*, which means "arrival," "appearance," or "coming." Christians celebrate the season of Advent in recognition of Jesus' arrival at Christmas. Traditionally the four weeks before Christmas are set aside to prepare for his arrival.

It is my hope that *Christmas with Luke* will help you in your Advent preparations as you prepare for Christ's arrival.

While not following the Advent calendar strictly, this book will lead you and your family on a twenty-five-day journey to Christmas. Each day we will read one chapter from the gospel of Luke. On December 25 we will return to Luke 2 to read the well-known Christmas narrative.

Christmas with Luke follows the December Scripture readings from *The Climb* (see description in the back of the book), but there is a unique devotional article from each chapter of Luke that has specific application for this season. *Christmas with Luke* also has questions to help you apply the scripture and devotional thoughts to your Christmas preparations. Finally, activities and questions for children and families are provided for each day.

HOW TO USE
Christmas with Luke

Since the dates of Advent change each year, this book is structured around the days of the month. Beginning on December 1, daily Scripture readings and devotional articles lead you to Christmas Day. On December 25 you will return to Luke 2:1–20 to read the well-known Christmas story as part of your Christmas Day celebration.

It is suggested that you use *Christmas with Luke* separate from your regular daily devotions. Perhaps you have your personal devotions in the mornings. In that case you could use *Christmas with Luke* in the evenings. Or if your daily quiet time is in the evening, then consider using this book during suppertime or right after.

It is important to give yourself and your family enough time to allow the Holy Spirit to speak to you as you work through the materials. It will probably take you anywhere from ten to twenty minutes to complete each day. You can dedicate more time if you wish. Here is a suggested outline:

1. Read the chapter from Luke. On December 1 it will be Luke 1, on December 2 it will be Luke 2, and so on. This can be done earlier in the day and/ or individually if that helps with your family dynamics.

2. Read the scripture focus found before the devotional article. You may consider having everybody read this in unison.

3. Read the article together. If there are two or more people, you can read aloud, alternating paragraphs or taking turns from day to day.

4. Recite the prayer found on the next page. If you're with others, have everyone recite it together. If young children are present, do a short paraphrase for the children to repeat.

5. Discuss the questions found in "Consider."

6. If desired, discuss and reflect upon the items in "For Further Study and Reflection."

7. If you have children, complete the activity and discussion found in "For Kids and Families." If time is limited, you may want to choose this option over the other discussion options ("Consider" and "For Further Study and Reflection"). Hint: Parents will want to look at these items beforehand in order to prepare.

8. If you miss a day, don't panic! On the next day stay with the schedule without trying to make it up. The articles are not dependent upon each other,

and there is even some repetition of ideas for rein- forcement. (You may want to designate a time to make up the ones you've missed, such as a Sunday evening or even on a day after Christmas.)

Are you ready to journey to *Christmas with Luke*? Let's get started!

DECEMBER 1

Are You Sure?

Read Luke 1

*". . . that you may have certainty concerning
the things you have been taught."* (Luke 1:4)

A t a young age I learned basic spiritual truths from my mom and others. As an older child I had intermittent involvement in and instruction from the Church of Christ in Montpelier, Ohio. As a young teen I received Christ as my Savior at the altar of the Pioneer, Ohio, Church of the Nazarene. After that, my spiritual instruction began in earnest. For the ensuing forty-six years I have been taught by pastors and laypeople, professors and friends. I have read commentaries, books, and periodicals. I have attended seminars and conferences, listened to webcasts and CDs. I have been taught many, many things.

I desperately need "certainty concerning the things [I] have been taught."

In a changing world with evolving morals, how can we be sure of what is right? It seems that what once was right is now wrong, and the wrong from yesterday is right today. Is there a source of knowledge that will withstand the changing culture? Is there some foundation on which I can build my life with confidence?

Yes, there is! The Holy Spirit inspired a medical doctor—his name was Luke—to write a book for that very purpose. That book is the gospel of Luke, and it is one of the sixty-six books of the Bible. In the modern deluge of relativism and pluralism, the Bible stands as the unchanging source of truth. When everything else collapses, the Word of God remains constant.

One of the things I learned as a child was the words to a familiar chorus: "The B - I - B - L - E—yes, that's the Book for me. I stand alone on the Word of God: the B - I - B - L - E!"

Prayer: Thank you, Lord, for your Word, for there I find Jesus; I find life. Grant that in the noise and confusion of this world I will be able to see and follow your Word with certainty and hope. In Christ's name. Amen.

Consider: Are there things in the Bible you don't understand? What?

What are some things in the Bible that you struggle to accept? To live by? Do you need to do anything about these things? What?

What are some current events and cultural trends that are in opposition to biblical teaching? How should you respond to these trends?

How can you be certain in your faith?

For Further Study and Reflection: Research how the Bible was written.

Reflect: Does this information change your understanding of and response to God's Word? How?

For Kids and Families: Go on a hunt through your house to see how many Bibles you can find. Count them. Look at them and compare them.

Discuss:
- Why is the Bible such an important book?
- How does the Bible affect your life?

DECEMBER 2

Oh, While You're Here...

Read Luke 2

"And while they were there . . ." (Luke 2:6)

In *The God Who Comes* Carlo Carretto writes, "The best metaphor for our world of today is astronauts speeding through the cosmos. . . . But the Church resembles Mary and Joseph traveling from Egypt to Nazareth on a donkey, holding in their arms the weakness and poverty of the Child Jesus: God incarnate."

Although this journey to Nazareth is from Matthew's account, the journey to Bethlehem in Luke is similar. Everything about that journey indicated their powerlessness and poverty:

- forced to travel eighty miles (five to ten days) while pregnant

- separated from comforts, safety, and family when they would rather be home

- compelled to take "unpaid leave"

- all for the "privilege" of paying their taxes!

Yet "while they were there" something happened that changed the course of history! This event changed your life and mine and the lives of countless others. Hope was born "while they were there."

Today we value going fast, being comfortable, getting noticed, and wielding power. In the story of Jesus' birth we learn that God sees things differently. In the slow, weary, painful steps of a very pregnant teenager and her frustrated husband, God chose to reveal himself.

Where are you this Christmas season? Most of us live the plodding, painful lives depicted by Joseph and Mary's journey. Our lives are uneventful and unnoticed, insignificant and inadequate. But remember: while you are here—just where you are—God comes.

———— ✳ ————

Prayer: Thank you, Lord, that you chose to come to a humble couple in an insignificant place. In your arrival there you have hallowed lives as plain and ordinary as mine. Come into my heart, Lord Jesus!

Consider: What difficult circumstances in your life right now resemble the plodding journey of Joseph and Mary to Bethlehem? What good thing(s) might be born from these hard situations?

Who do you know whose life might be described as a plodding journey? How can you help or encourage him or her?

For Further Study and Reflection: Why do you think Luke focused on Jesus' birth more than any other gospel writer did? What do we learn in Matthew, Mark, and John that Luke does not tell us about?

Reflect: What do the differences and omissions suggest about the birth narrative?

For Kids and Families: We all like to have fun! Go find your favorite toy. Share with your family why you like to play with it.

Discuss:
- What makes this toy fun for you?
- What is something you *don't* find fun?
- Do you think it was fun for Mary and Joseph to walk so far to Bethlehem?
- What makes it easier to accomplish tasks that aren't fun?

DECEMBER 3

Baby Jesus or Baptizing Jesus?

Read Luke 3

"He will baptize you with the Holy Spirit and fire."
(Luke 3:16)

The arrival of Jesus was quite an affair: heralded by angels, witnessed by shepherds, attended by wise men, rejected by rulers. But the baby who caused this stir fell silent. After thirty years the silence was broken by "a voice of one calling in the wilderness" (v. 4).

That voice calling was, of course, that of John the Baptist. He created quite a stir himself—gathering great crowds, baptizing repentant sinners, and disturbing religious pretenders. John said of Jesus and himself, however, "He must increase, but I must decrease" (John 3:30). Why? Because

John knew that he merely baptized with water for repentance, while Jesus would baptize with the Holy Spirit.

Jesus, the Babe of Bethlehem, is the one who—

- **Baptizes** with the Holy Spirit and fire. Gone is the weakness of the Babe of Bethlehem. Jesus offers the power of the Holy Spirit to those who follow him.

- **Clears** his threshing floor. The wheat and the chaff exist together on the threshing floor. But the floor will be cleared. The winnowing fork of judgment will separate the evil from the good.

- **Gathers** the wheat into his barn but burns the chaff. The separation of wheat from chaff will result in a gathering and a burning. The judge? Jesus! Those who have accepted Christ will be gathered to be with him forever. Those who have rejected him will be blown away on the winds of a godless eternity.

Don't leave Jesus in the manger this Christmas season. Make him the Lord of your life.

———— ✵ ————

Prayer: Jesus, this Christmas season help me to remember that you are more than a baby in a manger. You are the almighty Son of God and the Judge of all. I humbly bow before you in worship and surrender. In your name I pray. Amen.

Consider: Which is easier for the world to accept—the baby Jesus or the baptizing Jesus? Why?

Are there things Jesus wants to clear from your life? What are they?

For Further Study and Reflection: What do you think it means to be baptized with fire? With the Holy Spirit?

What do you learn about Spirit baptism in Acts 1–2?

Reflect: Read Acts 19:1–6. Have you received the Holy Spirit since you believed?

For Kids and Families: Look at some baby pictures of people in your family. Think about how the people in the pictures have changed.

Discuss:

- What are some examples of things you can do now that you couldn't do when you were a baby?
- What kinds of things will you be able to do when you become an adult that can you cannot do now?
- How can Jesus help you grow into the kind of person he wants you to be?

DECEMBER 4

It Means What?

Read Luke 4

"And they rose up and drove him out of the town."
(Luke 4:29)

In our secular society "Merry Christmas" has become less frequent, replaced by the politically correct "Happy Holidays." Christ has been driven out of Christmas!

We're not surprised. It happened in the Bible. In Luke 4, Jesus was driven from Nazareth. At first the Nazarenes loved this hometown boy who was "all the rage" around the country. Perhaps they hoped he could turn around their sorry reputation. But when Jesus called them out on their spiritual deadness, they decided they didn't like him after all. They drove him out. More than that, they "drove him out . . . so that they could throw him down the cliff" (v. 29). They were mad!

People are still mad at Jesus. They don't like him calling out their sin. So they drive him out. Jesus is okay in churches' manger scenes, but we won't tolerate a manger scene on public property. We may let him slip into a song or two during the season, but it's best if his name doesn't come up. Throughout the year Jesus can't come to our schools nor can he be part of our conversations at work. God forbid that he would show up in any public forums. So—"Happy Holidays!"

But just as in Luke 4, Jesus has the last laugh. He walked right through their midst and went on his way. Today I think I can hear him laughing when people say, "Happy Holidays," because in these substitute words he is still right there in their midst—*holiday* derives from the old English *haligdæg*, literally "a day consecrated to *divine* purposes." I like that. They are saying it's his day!

So when you hear, "Happy Holidays!" don't be offended. Just smile and say, "Merry Christmas!

Prayer: Lord, thank you for the holy and happy celebration of Christmas. Help me to spread the joy of this season everywhere I go. In your name I pray. Amen.

Consider: Have you ever felt intimidated about or been restricted from saying, "Merry Christmas"? What were the circumstances? How did you feel? What should you feel in situations like that?

What does Christmas mean in *your* life and family? How do you celebrate Christmas? What message do your celebrations convey?

For Further Study and Reflection: Read Matthew 2 to discover and discuss how the wise men and Joseph reacted to negative reactions to the arrival of Jesus.

Reflect: Does that change how you feel about today's cultural climate? How? What should you do differently?

For Kids and Families: Use a computer to look up how to say, "Merry Christmas," in other languages.

Discuss:

- Why do you think some people may be afraid to say, "Merry Christmas"?
- How can you spread the joy of Christmas to others this year?

DECEMBER 5

The Old Is Good

Read Luke 5

"And no one after drinking old wine desires new,
for he says, 'The old is good.'" (Luke 5:39)

When Jesus came preaching the good news of God's grace, many opposed his message. They just didn't get it. For generations they had been drinking the old wine of the law. It was good. The new wine of grace did not appeal to them. "We are doing just fine, thank you!"

There were others, however, "tax collectors and sinners," who gladly received the new wine of the kingdom. They were sick and tired of what sin was doing to them and to their families. They welcomed Jesus and his message, for they recognized that they were sick and needed a physician. Repenting of their past sins, they drank deeply of God's grace. "Lord, be merciful to me, a sinner!"

It is easy, even after drinking the new wine of grace, to fall back into the habit of saying, "The old is good." As we walk with the Lord we grow accustomed to doing things a certain way. God likes to surprise us from time to time: "Behold, I am doing a new thing" (Isaiah 43:19).

That's what Christmas was—a *new* thing: "Behold, I bring you good *news* of great joy." This season is a good time to remind ourselves that God is continually doing something new and that we should be open to doing something new as well. "We've always done it that way!" should be replaced with "God, what new thing are you going to do in my life today?"

———— ✳ ————

Prayer: God of creativity and life, I kneel before the Babe of Bethlehem and pray that the kingdom would be born in me—new and fresh—today. Help me to drink deeply of the new wine of grace day by day. In Christ's name I pray. Amen.

Consider: What new thing is God doing in my life right now? Am I cooperating or resisting?

What old ways am I holding on to in—

- worshiping?
- witnessing?
- serving?

Is God speaking to me about making changes in these areas?

For Further Study and Reflection: Do an Internet search on different forms of Christian worship around the world. Consider if some are "wrong" and others are "right."

Reflect: Read Acts 2:41–47 and 1 Corinthians 11 and 14 and consider first-century Christian worship. How is worship different today? Read John 4:24. What is the "true way" to worship?

For Kids and Families: Try a new food together as a family.

Discuss:

- Why are people sometimes afraid to try new foods?
- Why are people afraid to let God do something new in their lives?
- What new thing could you try to get closer to God during this Christmas season?

DECEMBER 6

Give Me Your Poor

Read Luke 6

*"Blessed are you who are poor, for yours is
the kingdom of God."* (Luke 6:20)

"Give me your tired, your poor,
Your huddled masses yearning to breathe free,
The wretched refuse of your teeming shore.
Send these, the homeless, tempest-tossed to me,
I lift my lamp beside the golden door!"

These words of hope by Emma Lazarus are found on the base of the Statue of Liberty in New York Harbor. Good news! For the exile there is a home. I have read accounts of those arriving from distant lands and dark lives. Upon seeing Lady Liberty for the first time, they are overcome with emotion. They are indeed blessed.

Jesus longs to bless the poor, tired, huddled masses. But unlike the Statue of Liberty, he doesn't simply stand beside heaven's golden door waiting to welcome those who might somehow find their way. No, Jesus *came to* the homeless exiles—to those longing for a place and for freedom—that he might lead them to the kingdom of God.

And it doesn't matter that we are poor. As a matter of fact, Jesus said that the poor are blessed, for it is the poor who receive the kingdom he gives. There is no other way that we can enter. We must receive this gift by faith.

This season remember that Jesus left the riches of heaven to be born in a cattle stall. He came to our poverty that we might be welcomed into his kingdom. A star shines over a stable in Bethlehem and he has come to show you the way home.

Prayer: Thank you, Father, for "the grace of our Lord Jesus Christ, that though he was rich, yet for [our] sake he became poor, so that [we] by his poverty might become rich" (2 Corinthians 8:9). In Jesus' name I pray. Amen.

Consider: Research the wealthiest areas of the United States or the world or consider the wealthiest people you know. Are those people the happiest compared to those in other regions?

In what ways are you poor? How does poverty impact your happiness? In what ways are you rich? How does your wealth shape your happiness?

In what ways is it easier to be happy when you are poor? How does Proverbs 13:8 impact your answer?

For Further Study and Reflection: Read Matthew 19:16–30. What did Jesus mean when he said that it is easier for a camel to go through the eye of a needle than for a rich person to enter the kingdom of heaven?

Reflect: Are material things impeding your celebration of Christmas? How? What should you do about it?

For Kids and Families: Decide as individuals or as a family on something you already own that you could give to someone who is in need.

Discuss:

- How does it make you feel to give away something you really like?
- How does it make you feel to know that Jesus gave up the riches of heaven to be born in a dark and dirty stable?

DECEMBER 7

The One

Read Luke 7

*"Are you the one who is to come, or shall
we look for another?"* (Luke 7:20)

Day after day the mail carrier came and went. "It"
wasn't in the box. The UPS truck drove up the
street, but the driver passed right on by. The
FedEx truck pulled into the driveway and left packages,
but "the one" was not on the porch. Christmas was quickly
approaching and the special gift I had ordered for my wife
was not yet here. I kept looking.

"The blind receive their sight, the lame walk . . . the deaf
hear, the dead are raised up, the poor have good news
preached to them" (v. 22). This was Jesus' response to a des-

perate John the Baptist, who was locked in Herod's prison and left asking, "*Are you the One, or should I keep looking?*"

In addition to citing the evidence, Jesus admonished John: "Blessed is the one who is not offended by me" (v. 23). Not *offended* by Jesus? John had tied his fortunes to Jesus! He had dedicated his life to preparing the way for Jesus. He had lived in the desert, worn itchy camel hair, and eaten crunchy locusts—all for the sake of Jesus. How could Jesus insinuate that John was offended by him?

The Greek root of *offended* is *skandalon* and means literally "a snare, stumbling-block, cause for error." So perhaps a better way to understand what Jesus said would be "Blessed is the one who does not stumble on account of me." Jesus knew how hard it was for John and was reminding him, "Don't get discouraged over the circumstances. They may not seem to point to me, but remember: I am the One."

Perhaps this Christmas season circumstances seem to be against you. Keep up your courage. Keep looking. Jesus *is* the One.

———— ✦ ————

Prayer: Lord, sometimes it's hard for us to see and understand your purposes, but in Christmas you have made your love very clear to us. You are the One. Help us to look no further. In your name we pray. Amen.

Consider: What "prisons" are holding you back and discouraging your faith? Are they of your own making or caused by another? What hope and encouragement does Christmas bring to you?

Whom do you know who is discouraged in his or her faith? What can you do or say to help this person?

For Further Study and Reflection: Read Genesis 50:15–21. What was "all the evil" that Joseph's brothers had caused him? (See Genesis 37–41.)

How did Joseph respond? (See Genesis 50:20.)

Reflect: What is your "go-to" attitude when discouraging things happen? When they persist? What, if anything, needs to change?

For Kids and Families: Play the "shell game" as a family. Turn three opaque cups upside down and hide a small object (marble, bottle cap, or so on) under one cup. Move the cups around quickly to mix them up and let others guess which cup is hiding the object.

Discuss:
- How did you feel when you guessed correctly? Incorrectly?
- How can we stay focused on seeing God at work in our lives even when things get confusing?

DECEMBER 8

Water from the Rock

Read Luke 8

"And some fell on the rock, and as it grew up, it withered away, because it had no moisture." (Luke 8:6)

"These two trees were planted at the same time." I didn't believe my friend Marshall when he told me that. One tree, over ten feet tall, was laden with beautiful red apples. The other, barely reaching five feet, was scrawny and completely devoid of apples. My friend pointed to the scrawny tree and said, "That one was planted over a rock." Beneath the surface—just a little deeper than Marshall had dug the hole—there was a huge rock that prevented the tree from taking deep root. It had no significant moisture.

Jesus' parable in Luke 8 describes what happens to seed that has no moisture. Some seed falls on the path where it never gets down into the moist, fertile soil. Other seed falls among weeds where the weeds suck the soil dry. And some seed falls on rocky ground where, as with my friend's apple tree, the moisture is shallow and short-lived.

Christmas joy is like that. It requires "moisture." Some people miss it because life is a hardened path of sorrow, suffering, and suspicion. Circumstances rob them of hope and faith. Others miss Christmas joy because of the "weeds." All the parties, decorating, shopping, and cooking suck the joy right out. Still others miss Christmas joy because their lives are shallow and shortsighted. There is precious little depth to collect and hold the meaning of Christmas.

Plant the seeds of your Christmas celebration in the rich, moist soil of Jesus Christ. Like Moses' rock in the wilderness, Jesus is the Rock that will pour forth life-giving, refreshing water. Drink deeply of Jesus yourself this Christmas and lead others to the fountain!

Prayer: Jesus, you are Living Water. You came to this earth to bring us joy and peace, hope and love. Help me in the midst of the hustle and bustle of this season to drink deeply of the water of life. In your name I pray. Amen.

Consider: Are there weeds sucking the joy out of your heart this Christmas season? What are they?

Is it time to do some weeding?

For Further Study and Reflection: Read Exodus 17:1–8 and Numbers 20:1–13. Where did that water come from?

Now read 1 Corinthians 10:1–4. How does that change your answer?

Reflect: What is the source of your Christmas joy?

For Kids and Families: Look together carefully at a Christmas tree, either in your home or somewhere else. Examine the different and varied ornaments, their intricacies, and other features.

Discuss:
- Which ornament is your favorite? Why do you like it?
- How do Christmas decorations bring joy to our celebrations?
- How can we always remember the importance of the birth of Jesus?
- How joyful were Mary and Joseph when Jesus was born?

DECEMBER 9

Intentions or Actions?

Read Luke 9

"I will follow you, Lord, but . . ." (Luke 9:61)

On a mission trip to Guatemala our trip coordinator, Matt, was very specific: "When we're in the airport in Guatemala, follow me!" I really meant to—I just got distracted! Matt was not happy that my intentions and actions didn't match.

As Jesus was preaching the gospel, he encountered three men with intentions to follow him. One by one, however, they came up with excuses not to follow him.

- The first man apparently had some concern about their accommodations. That's legitimate. We need to make sure that we are well-rested for the work of the kingdom! But Jesus wouldn't guarantee his comfort.

- The second wanted to bury his father. That sounds legitimate until you consider the fact that the man's father was probably still alive! What he was saying was "Lord, after my father dies and gives me my inheritance, I'll catch up with you." Jesus told him that the kingdom doesn't wait on our convenience.

- The third man with good intentions wanted to say goodbye to his family. Surely that's okay! But Jesus, looking into his heart, read his true intentions. The man couldn't let go of the familiar and would always yearn to return. Jesus told him to make a clean break.

Compare these three men with good intentions to the three wise men, whose actions spoke more loudly than their words. They left safety and comfort, family and friends when they set out to find the one "born King of the Jews." They followed the Christmas star all the way to "the place where the child was . . . and offered him gifts, gold and frankincense and myrrh" (Matthew 2). This season do your intentions translate into actions? Are you following Jesus?

———— ✳ ————

Prayer: Lord, at Christmas my thoughts go to you more readily and frequently, and I have good intentions to follow you, but my actions don't always reflect my intentions. Help me to follow you not just at Christmas but *every* day. In Christ's name I pray. Amen.

Consider: How have I said, "Not now, Lord, but later I will. . . ." to Jesus?

Are there intentions that I need to turn into actions? What are they?

For Further Study and Reflection: Read Philippians 3:12–16. What from my past do I need to forget? To what in my future do I need to press on?

Reflect: In 1 Kings 20:11 the king of Israel said, "Let not him who straps on his armor boast himself as he who takes it off." Am I boasting prematurely of accomplishments yet to be completed?

For Kids and Families: Play a game of "Follow the Leader" together. Allow each member of the family to take a turn at being the leader. Encourage play and creativity (skipping, hopping, jumping, and so on).

Discuss:

- How well would this game work if the people who were supposed to be following didn't follow?
- What kinds of problems might we have if we don't follow Jesus?

DECEMBER 10

Work and Worship

Read Luke 10

*"Mary has chosen the good portion, which will not
be taken away from her."* (Luke 10:42)

Last week Lana and I took time out of our schedule to attend our district Christmas banquet. Even though we are retired now, it is still a busy time of the year. Our kids and grandkids are coming in a few days and we have to get ready! It would have been easy to say, "Let's not go to the banquet this year. We have too much to do." I'm glad we went, though. We were blessed by the fellowship but especially by the Christmas concert, which was part of the program. As we worshiped, we enjoyed the presence of the Lord.

There are lots of things that can distract us from the presence of the Lord at Christmas. Isn't that sad? They are good things—just like the things Martha was doing: cooking, cleaning, hosting. But Jesus wants us to be *with* him, to sit at his feet, to worship. That's the "good portion" that he said Mary had chosen.

The word translated *portion* indicates "a part as distinct from the whole." There is indeed more to being his disciple than worship. There is work to be done. The work that Martha had chosen to do was not unimportant nor was it unrelated to being a faithful disciple. But as Mary's worship was just a part, so also Martha's work was just a part. Worship, however, was the best part, the "good portion." If we have to choose between one or the other, we should choose the good part, shouldn't we? If we have to choose which to do first, we should worship before we work if possible.

This Christmas in the midst of all the work of serving the Lord, spend time in worship—sitting at his feet.

Prayer: Thank you, Lord, for Mary and Martha, who show me that being your disciple is a combination of work and worship. Help me to do both this season and all year long. In Christ's name I pray. Amen.

Consider: In what ways are you like Martha? In what ways are you like Mary?

Do you need to make adjustments to bring balance into your work and worship?

For Further Study and Reflection: Think about the retail workers, delivery service providers, and even your church ministers and workers. At Christmas their work is increased. What can you do to help ease their load and brighten their holiday?

Reflect: Read Matthew 11:27–30. Do you need rest for your *soul*?

For Kids and Families: Let's put this into practice! Take some time to worship together as a family (pray together, sing some Christmas songs, and so on). Then jump in and as a group accomplish a simple task that needs to be done around the house (decorate the tree, bake cookies, or so on).

Discuss:
- Why is worship important?
- Why is work important?
- Why is it important to worship before we work?

DECEMBER 11

The Enchanted Forest

Read Luke 11

"Therefore be careful lest the light in you be darkness."
(Luke 11:35)

I love Christmas lights! I have carefully arranged nine Christmas "trees" in my side yard, each with hundreds of lights. I call it "the Enchanted Forest." I have three more "trees" of lights on my front porch. Then there are lights on two trees flanking the front of the house. I love coming over the hill after dark and seeing all the lights! It makes me feel so festive! The other night when I topped the hill, however, I was disappointed. There were no twinkling lights to greet me! I discovered that moisture had gotten into one of the timers and the circuit had been tripped. I took immediate action, covering the timer so that it wouldn't get wet in the future. After all, I hadn't done all that work to let the lights be dark.

During this season we are surrounded by lights. In addition to lights on trees, there are luminescent inflatables in front yards, stars atop trees, candles in windows, and luminaries along sidewalks and driveways. With all these lights, one would think that darkness would be kept at bay. I wonder, though, if these lesser lights obscure the true Light of Christmas.

Jesus said that we must "be careful lest the light in you be darkness." I think those words are especially relevant at Christmastime. We should be even more diligent at Christmas to make sure that the Light of the World is shining brightly in us. All the parties, gifts, and decorations should open our eyes to the glorious truth that God's Son came to earth to save us from our sins.

This Christmas may Jesus shine not only *in* you also but *through* you so that others may see and come to the Light.

Prayer: Lord, thank you that you have shone your light in my life. This Christmas season help me to let my light shine so that others may come to you. In Jesus' name I pray. Amen.

Consider: Have you ever seen the light of Jesus in someone? What was that person like?

Consider times in your life when your light shone the most brightly. What was happening in those times? Is your light shining that brightly now?

For Further Study and Reflection: Go online and explore the history of Christmas decorations in various times and places—both Christian cultures and non-Christian cultures. What do these various decorations symbolize?

Reflect: How should I "decorate" my life to symbolize the true meaning of Christmas in this season and throughout the year?

For Kids and Families: Look at Christmas lights in your neighborhood (or online) together. Discuss and enjoy the different displays.

Discuss:
- Which light display was your favorite? Why?
- What kinds of things distract us from the true light of Christmas?

DECEMBER 12

Oil and Water

Read Luke 12

"Do you think that I have come to give peace on earth?
No, I tell you, but rather division." (Luke 12:51)

"For to us a child is born, to us a son is given . . . and his name shall be called . . . Prince of Peace" (Isaiah 9:6). "Glory to God in the highest, and on earth peace" (Luke 2:14). The apostle Paul identified Jesus as "the Lord of peace" (2 Thessalonians 3:16) and said that "he himself is our peace" (Ephesians 2:14).

In this day of political animus and personal anxiety, we hear prophet and angel, preacher and apostle all alike say that Jesus brings peace. Why then did Jesus say, "Do you think that I have come to give peace on earth?"

The world defines peace as the absence of conflict. But the peace of Jesus is different from that of the world: "Peace I leave with you; my peace I give to you. Not as the world gives do I give to you" (John 14:27). "In the world you will have tribulation. But take heart; I have overcome the world" (John 16:33).

Jesus himself is actually a threat to the world's type of peace:

- Christians are compelled to bear witness while the world seeks to silence Christ.

- Christians operate under different ethics and values, bringing the kingdom of God into conflict with the kingdoms of men.

As they say, "Oil and water don't mix."

Jesus dwelling within us, however, gives us a peace that passes understanding. Our circumstances may not be peaceful, but our hearts can be at peace, for the One born in Bethlehem is the Prince of Peace. So even when differences cause division, we have "peace with God through our Lord Jesus Christ" (Romans 5:1).

——— ✳ ———

Prayer: "O God our Father, who didst send forth thy Son to be King of kings and Prince of peace: Grant that all the kingdoms of this world may become the kingdom of Christ, and learn of him the way of peace. Send forth among all people the spirit of good will and reconciliation" (*The Book of Worship*).

Consider: How has being a Christian caused conflict in your life?

Think of ways that Christianity clashes with popular culture. How should we respond?

For Further Study and Reflection: Read John 18:33–40. What did Jesus mean when he said, "My kingdom is not of this world" (v. 36)? How should we respond to that?

Reflect: Do you ever find yourself "waging war according to the flesh" (2 Corinthians 10:3)? If so, what should you do?

For Kids and Families: Try an experiment! Pour a small amount of oil and water together in a bowl or jar. Allow the children to try to mix them together. Discuss the fact that this just doesn't work. (Tip: Try coloring the water to make the effect more pronounced.)

Discuss:
- What happened when you tried to mix the oil and water together?

- What are some examples of things in life that just don't mix (school rivals, people who disagree, and so on)?

- What do you think about Jesus' ability to bring peace to our hearts even when something that's not peaceful is going on around us?

DECEMBER 13

Leaven Me Alone!

Read Luke 13

"It is like leaven that a woman took and hid in three measures of flour, until it was all leavened."
(Luke 13:21)

I enjoy saying, "Merry Christmas," to people and seeing their reactions. Some people return my Christmas greeting. Others say, "Happy Holidays." Still others don't respond at all. Those are the ones I'm really interested in—how I can get the Christmas spirit into them.

The words *Merry Christmas* are like the leaven "that a woman took and hid in three measures of flour." This season gives us opportunity to put a little leaven (yeast) into our community, to lift it above the crass commercialism that abounds. But let's go beyond those words and mix in "three measures of flour, until it [is] all leavened."

Think about these three measures to go with your "Merry Christmas"—

- *Peace*. Things are busier than usual in this season. The pace is hectic. Nerves are raw. Patience grows thin. Instead of expressing impatience, do something to promote peace.

- *Hope*. Some people experience painful memories and loneliness. Give hope this year. Try going to a nursing home and singing carols. Invite somebody to lunch. Let people know that they are not forgotten.

- *Joy*. Many have seemingly lost their ability to smile. Have some fun at Christmas. Decorate and celebrate. After all, this is a birthday party, and nobody wants a sourpuss at a birthday party. Smile!

Don't hide the real meaning of Christmas in your heart. Mix it in with the world around you until it is all leavened.

———— ✴ ————

Prayer: Lord, in this season of Christmas I tend to get focused on what I have to get done. Help me instead to bring a "Merry Christmas"—mixed with peace, hope, and joy—to those around me. In your name I pray. Amen.

Consider: How can you leaven your workplace, your family, your neighborhood, or your classroom with Christmas joy?

Do you know someone who has experienced loss this year? What will you do to help this person rediscover the hope of Christmas?

For Further Study and Reflection: Read Ecclesiastes 11:1–2. What do you think it means to "cast your bread upon the waters"? How will it return to you?

Reflect: Recent fads have extolled "paying it forward" or "random acts of kindness." What may be wrong about those sentiments? How could they be improved?

For Kids and Families: Provide paper and crayons (or other art materials) for making Christmas cards. Encourage the children to focus on peace, hope, and joy as they decorate the cards. Then spread the spirit of the season to others by personally delivering the cards to someone who may need uplifting.

Discuss:
- How did the cards you designed reflect peace, hope, and joy?
- What did you think about the reactions of the people who received them?

DECEMBER 14

Pass the Salt, Please

Read Luke 14

"Salt is good, but if salt has lost its taste, how shall its saltiness be restored?" (Luke 14:34)

I love making caramel corn at Christmas. One year I forgot to add the salt—it was just a small amount—to the recipe. The caramel corn "lost its taste" without salt!

Salt is an important ingredient in many dishes. Jesus used the significance of salt to teach his disciples that their lives needed to be flavored by the kingdom of God and its values.

Let's make sure we add a little salt to our Christmas celebrations this year, for—

- *Salt preserves.* In ancient times salt was used to keep foods fresh and edible. How can we add a little salt to preserve Christmas, to keep its true meaning fresh?

- *Salt flavors.* Let's face it: almost everything from french fries to broccoli tastes better with some salt. Even our desserts—such as caramel corn!—include a small amount of salt to bring out the other flavors. In the midst of all the other "tastes" of Christmas, let us flavor the Christmas season with its true significance: the birth of Jesus Christ.

- *Salt cleanses.* Salt was used to disinfect wounds. It was not a particularly pleasant experience to the one injured, but it was necessary to prevent infection. The message of sin and repentance is unpleasant to sinners, but that should not cause us to shy away from spreading the gospel at Christmastime.

Don't let the world's cynicism and consumerism rob you of the taste of Christmas. Instead, let your Christmas be salted with the true reason for the season. Pass the salt, please!

------ ✳ ------

Prayer: Jesus, help us to be salt and light to those around us this season. The world desperately needs you, even when they don't know it. Help us to act in a way that salts Christmas with your love, peace, and joy. In Christ's name we pray. Amen.

Consider: What are the three functions of salt described above?

How can I personally . . .
- Add a little "salt" to preserve the meaning of Christmas?
- Spread love and kindness in the place of consumerism this Christmas?
- Share the message of God's love and forgiveness?

For Further Study and Reflection: Where does salt come from? Does that help you understand Jesus' words in Mark 9:50—"Have salt in yourselves"?

Reflect: Research "covenant of salt" in the Bible. What does it mean and how does it apply to you?

For Kids and Families: Enjoy a salty snack together as a family (pretzels, popcorn, and so on). Talk about why salt has been added to the food and how it might taste without the salt.

Discuss:
- Do you like salt on your food?
- How is the salt on the food like the "salt" we should be in the world?
- What might happen if we lose our "saltiness"?

DECEMBER 15

Let's Have a Party!

Read Luke 15

*"What woman, having ten silver coins, if she loses
one coin, does not light a lamp and sweep the house and
seek diligently until she finds it?"* (Luke 15:8)

How upset we were when we lost sight of her at church that day! She was a guest in our home for a very special reason. She had decided with God's help to kick an addiction. She was staying with us to get a new start, away from triggers and temptations. But we got more than we bargained for. Not only was she a guest in our home, but she also quickly became a treasure in our hearts! So when she came up "missing," we became frantic! We searched the church and the grounds. I drove around town stopping at a few of the usual places. We diligently kept looking until we found her. How relieved we were when we were reunited!

Jesus described a lady who lost something valuable to her—a coin. It was likely part of her dowry and was probably worn as part of a headdress or necklace for safekeeping. It was close to her heart and mind. Yes, she had nine others, but every one of them was valuable to her. So when she lost this coin she searched diligently until she found it. And when she found it—she threw a party!

We are precious like that to God. Yes, he has many children, but he knows each one by name. He keeps us close to his heart and on his mind. When it comes to "finding" us, no effort is too great for him. That's why he sent his Son to a humble stable in Bethlehem—"to seek and to save the lost" (Luke 19:10). This Christmas remember that we are God's treasure, sought after and loved. Let's have a party!

———— ✳ ————

Prayer: Thank you, Lord Jesus, that you came to seek me and find me and save me. Oh, the wonderful love of my Savior! I rejoice that I am the focus of your attention and affection. I love you with all my heart and soul and mind and strength. In your name I pray. Amen.

Consider: When in the Bible did God first begin seeking the lost? When will he stop?

What can you do to help people find their way "home" to God?

For Further Study and Reflection: Who are "the lost" whom Jesus came to seek and to save (Luke 19:10)? Read John 3:16; 1 Timothy 2:4; 2 Peter 3:9; Revelation 22:17.

Reflect: In Genesis 4 we read the story of Cain and Abel. What can you learn about God's attitude toward the sinner from his interactions with Cain?

For Kids and Families: Play a game of "I Spy" together as a family. One member of the group picks out an object in the room, tells the group what color it is, and the others try to guess the object. Be sure to allow each child a chance to be both a "chooser" and a "guesser."

Discuss:
- How did it feel when you finally guessed the correct object during the game?

- Have you ever lost something that was important to you and then found it? How did you feel when you found it?

- Why do you think Jesus considers us so important that he came to earth to search for us?

DECEMBER 16

I Am That Beggar

Read Luke 16

"At his gate was laid a beggar named Lazarus."
(Luke 16:20, NIV)

"I am that beggar." Those were the first words that occurred to me when I read today's scripture.

Just as Lazarus the beggar was laid at the gate of a rich man, the Son of God came to this earth as a baby in Bethlehem, where he was a "beggar" himself. As with all other babies, Jesus was completely dependent upon his mother and father. Since that time Jesus has appeared again and again in the form of one beggar or another.

Leo Tolstoy wrote a short piece called "Where Love Is, God Is." As the story goes, Jesus spoke to Martin, a cobbler, in a dream saying, "Watch the street, Martin, for tomorrow I shall appear to you and you will receive me." The next day Martin awoke with great anticipation. As the story goes, Martin did receive guests three times as the day wore on— all beggars in one way or another. Martin helped them in a variety of ways. Martin, however, became more and more discouraged as Christ himself failed to appear. At the end of the day a voice and vision came to him: "Martin, those beggars you helped were me."

Day after day Jesus appears to us and waits for us to receive him. He doesn't do it with dazzling lights and trumpet blasts. He is not nearly so dramatic. He's not even as dramatic as Martin's three guests in Tolstoy's short story. Instead, he comes to us in the simple beggars around us, people needing acceptance and support, assistance and hope. Will we receive him? Will we make room for him in our hearts?

Hear the Babe of Bethlehem saying, "I am that beggar."

Prayer: Lord, too often I look for you to come with stars and shepherds and angels! This season help me to see you in every face and respond with a smile and a word of encouragement. In your name I pray. Amen.

Consider: Do you need to make room for Jesus in your Christmas celebrations?

Do you need to make room for Jesus in your life?

For Further Study and Reflection: When we receive Jesus, we receive his identity. What is the hardest part of Jesus' identity to take upon ourselves?

Reflect: How does it make you feel to refer to Jesus as "that beggar"? Are your spiritual sensitivities offended? Are you indignant? Read Matthew 25:31–46. How does that change your answer?

For Kids and Families: Encourage each member of the family to find an article of clothing he or she no longer needs and donate it to a local clothing pantry.

Discuss:
- How does it make you feel when you see someone begging for food or money?
- How do you think Jesus would want us to respond when we see someone in need?

DECEMBER 17

Rise and Go

Read Luke 17

"Rise and go your way; your faith has made you well."
(Luke 17:19)

The story of Jesus' birth concludes with the shepherds rising and going their way after having seen the Baby. When Jesus met Mary outside the empty tomb and she knelt before him, clasping his feet, he told her in essence to "rise and go." He sent her with a message to the other disciples. Here in Luke 17 Jesus healed ten lepers. One returned and "fell on his face at Jesus' feet, giving him thanks" (v. 16). Jesus' message to him was "Rise and go your way" (v. 19).

Jesus calls us to himself and receives us when we come. He invites us to get away and rest. He bids us to come and dine. He sits down to "sup with us." He receives our worship and our gratitude. But then his message to us becomes "Rise and go."

- **Rise.** The leper had lived defeated and rejected. That low living was over! When Jesus touches us he does not leave us down in the miry clay. He lifts us up and sets our feet on a solid rock. What is our response to him? Do we say, "No, I would rather stay right here in the mud"? We are more than conquerors through Jesus Christ! Our faith has made us well. After cleansing, are we living well?

- **Go.** The cleansed leper was not only to rise but also to "go his way." Part of living well is living with purpose. The leper had a way to go, and so do we. We are commissioned to tell others about him. There are people we alone are called to reach, jobs we alone are called to do. After worship are we going our way?

Yes, celebrate Christmas with joy and peace and gratitude. Then—remember to "rise and go"!

Prayer: O Lord, you have cleansed me from the sins of my past and have given me a new and victorious life. Help me to have enough faith to live it this day. Help me to rise and go in Jesus' name. In his name I pray. Amen.

Consider: In what ways do you need the healing touch of Jesus? Does this story give you hope?

Who are "the people you alone are called to reach"? Will you reach them? What are the jobs you alone are called to do? Will you do them?

For Further Study and Reflection: Research the disease of leprosy. Do you think it is surprising that only one leper returned to give Jesus thanks?

Reflect: Are there things in your life you have failed to thank God for? How can you give him thanks?

For Kids and Families: Play a brainstorming game. How many things can you think of that rise? (Examples: the sun, temperature, people in the morning, and so on.) How many things can you think of that go? (Examples: cars, time, people, and so on.)

Discuss:

- What is the relationship between *rising* and *going*?
- What did Jesus mean when he told people to do this?
- Where would Jesus want you to go?

DECEMBER 18

A Good Baby

Read Luke 18

"Why do you call me good? No one is good except God alone."
(Luke 18:19)

At Christmastime it is natural to think about Jesus as a baby. I wonder sometimes if he was a "good baby." You know the kind—never fussy, smiling and cooing all the time, eating well, never spitting up, and—this one really gets me—sleeping through the night! Those are always somebody *else's* babies!

Whether or not Jesus was a "good baby," years later he was addressed as a "good teacher" by a rich and powerful man. Jesus asked him, though, "Why do you call me good?" I wonder if his answer was affected by what he knew was about to happen to him on the cross. There were those in his day, as there were in Job's day and our day, who saw any weakness as a sign of sin and corruption. "The God who suffers" or "the dying God" would be anathema in that culture. And since God alone is unaffected by sickness and death, since God alone lives forever, God alone is good. I think Jesus challenged that definition of *good* and thereby our concept of God.

We have a tendency to label people according to our definition of *good*, don't we? And we also wonder what might be wrong with people who are suffering. But suffering is the picture that Jesus painted from his birth to his death. He took on our flesh, our weakness, and ultimately our mortality. Yet he is God. And God is good.

And here is the good news of a crying, dying Jesus. He brings the strength of God to our weakness and the goodness of God to our sin and the life of God to our death. By his stripes we are healed.

Prayer: Thank you, Lord, that you took on flesh in all its weakness and even in its death so that you might give me power and life. I receive your goodness, your life today. In your name I pray. Amen.

Consider: Have you ever been around a fussy baby? When? Was it pleasant?

Why do you think babies "fuss"? Do you think Jesus "fussed"?

For Further Study and Reflection: Think of some ways that Jesus' humanity was on display in the gospels. Did that make him sinful? (See Hebrews 4:15.)

Reflect: Read Isaiah 53. Jesus took our imperfection and our pain, making it his own. Why did he do it? Is that good?

For Kids and Families: Play the "compliment game" together. Start with one member of the family and have each member say something good about that person. Make sure everyone gets a turn at being complimented.

Discuss:
- What was your favorite compliment?
- What makes Jesus good?
- How can that affect your life?

———— ✳ ————

DECEMBER 19

Compare, Contrast, and Consider

Read Luke 19

"Blessed is the King who comes in the name of the Lord!
Peace in heaven and glory in the highest!" (Luke 19:38)

When Jesus was born in Bethlehem the angels sang, "Glory to God in the highest! Peace on earth! Good will to men!" Over thirty years later when Jesus came into Jerusalem, the crowd echoed those angels: "Blessed is the King who comes in the name of the Lord! Peace in heaven and glory in the highest!"

Compare and contrast:

- **Coming**. In weakness and vulnerability Jesus came, first as a baby to live, then as a lamb to die. His coming was with great singing on both occasions. The first song was sung by angels, the second by a great throng of earthly worshipers.

- **Crown**. The child Jesus was recognized by wise men as the "King of the Jews." When he came to Jerusalem, Jesus was recognized as a king. When Pilate sent him to be crucified, he crowned him, "Jesus of Nazareth. King of the Jews" (Luke 23:38).

- **Crowds**. With a few shepherds, "a multitude of the heavenly host prais[ed] God" (Luke 2:13). When he came to Jerusalem "the whole multitude of his disciples began to rejoice and praise God with a loud voice" (Luke 19:37). That multitude, however, soon turned against Jesus as "all cried out together, 'Away with this man'" (Luke 23:18).

- **Cries**. The weak cry of a baby in manger became the loud cries of a crowd and the final, victorious cry of a Savior: "It is finished" (John 19:30).

Consider:

This Jesus who came to Bethlehem and Jerusalem will come again. Then he will be crowned King of Kings and Lord of Lords. A great crowd around the throne will cry out, "Glory to God in the highest!"

————— ✳ —————

Prayer: Jesus, thank you that you did not stop short but completed your mission. From heaven to Bethlehem, from Galilee to Jerusalem, from the cross to the grave—and then from death to life! Give me grace, O Lord, to follow in your steps. In your name I pray. Amen.

Consider: Look back at the four things we compared and contrasted in the devotional:

- Coming
- Crown
- Crowds
- Cries

Where do you fit in with each one of them? Why?

For Further Study and Reflection: What is the most worshipful thing you do? Is it sincere?

Reflect: Read the description of heaven's worship found in Revelation 4–5. Based on how you worship now, will you fit in there?

For Kids and Families: Sing or listen to some favorite Christmas songs together. Discuss the words and the meanings of the songs as you sing or listen.

Discuss:

- Why are Christmas songs such an important part of this season?
- If Jesus were singing with you, which song do you think might be his favorite? Why?
- How can our lives "sing" as the angels do and as the crowds did as we live each day?

DECEMBER 20

Hey, Squirt!

Read Luke 20

"I will send my beloved son; perhaps they will respect him."
(Luke 20:13)

During football bowl season I love to see those home videos that show the players as youngsters. Who would think that that sixty-pound kid would become a two-hundred-sixty-pound menace? It's hard to get respect when you're just a squirt! But squirts can grow up to be geysers!

Switch to Luke 20. When some sharecroppers began defrauding the owner of the vineyard, he decided to take action. First he sent servants to collect the rent. When they were refused, the owner decided to send his son. But the sharecroppers took one look at the boy and said, "He's just a kid! Let's take him out!" Later they had to reckon with the wrath of the father. It didn't turn out well for them.

God decided to send his Son, too. He was born in weakness. He grew up poor and inconsequential. His enemies said, "He's just a kid. Let's take him out." And they did! He died in humiliation and apparent defeat. Behind the Son, however, was the power of the Father. The weakness of death became the power of resurrection. Those who reject the Son have to answer to the Father. Those who do not judge the Son as powerful will stand before the Judge of all the earth.

God sent his Son to be the Savior of the world. As a baby and a boy he was weak and unimpressive. Even as an adult he was crucified in weakness. But God did not desert him to the grave! On the third day the deep was opened and Jesus came bursting forth in triumph and power!

Yes, let's respect the Son, the Baby of Bethlehem, for he is beloved. And behind this Baby is the power of Almighty God!

Prayer: "I thank you, Father, Lord of heaven and earth, that you have hidden these things from the wise and understanding and revealed them to little children . . . for such was your gracious will" [Matthew 11:25–26]. In Jesus' name I pray. Amen.

Consider: When we are new Christians, how are we like physical babies? In what ways do we stay that way? In what ways do we outgrow it?

Think of some people you have known who seemed to outgrow their potential. What made the difference in their lives that they could exceed expectations?

For Further Study and Reflection: Read the story of Shadrach, Meshach, and Abednego in Daniel 3. Pay attention to their "if not" in verse 18. Can you say, "If not," in your situation?

Reflect: In what circumstances of your life are you awaiting a resurrection? Will you trust God as you wait?

For Kids and Families: Have a little fun with a family "thumb wrestling" tournament. If you don't know what thumb wrestling is, you can find videos online to explain it. See who has the most "thumb power."

Discuss:

- Which family member has the most "thumb power"?
- Jesus didn't thumb wrestle his enemies, so how did he display his power over them?
- How can the power of God help you?

DECEMBER 21

You Were Always on My Mind

Read Luke 21

"And then they will see the Son of Man coming in a cloud with power and great glory." (Luke 21:27)

In the movie *A Christmas Story* thoughts of a Red Ryder BB gun consume Ralphie. He plans and plots how he can make sure it will be under the tree at Christmas. It's all he has on his mind.

What's on your mind this Christmas? Theologian A. W. Tozer wrote, "What comes into our minds when we think about God is the most important thing about us." The idea behind this has never been more needed than at Christmas, when so many have forgotten the true meaning of the holiday.

In Luke 21 Jesus shared some prophetic insights that may seem out of place at Christmas: wars, famine, earthquakes, and signs from heaven. He also foretold the martyrdom of believers who are called to give witness before kings. In the final days people will be "fainting with fear and with foreboding of what is coming on the world. For the powers of the heavens will be shaken" (v. 26). Then "they will see the Son of Man coming in a cloud with power and great glory" (v. 27). All will come face to face with Jesus. All will eventually bow to the name of Jesus and confess him as Lord (Philippians 2:10–11).

In Jesus' first coming over two thousand years ago there were those unwilling to confess him as Lord. Instead, they sought to find and eliminate a helpless baby. At the end of his life they arrested him and crucified him. But he rose from the dead and ascended to the Father! Soon he will come again "in a cloud with power and great glory."

—————— ✳ ——————

Prayer: Lord, how we long for the day when you come back to reclaim your children and to make all things new! Help us to look toward that day with excitement as your Son is revealed in all his power and glory. In your wonderful name we pray. Amen.

Consider: What are your favorite aspects of Christmas? What is on your mind this Christmas? What *should* be?

Read Acts 20:35. Why do you think that Jesus said it is more blessed to give than to receive?

For Further Study and Reflection: Make a list of the signs in Luke 21. How are these in evidence today?

Reflect: As you celebrate his first coming, may his second coming fill you with hope and peace, for the Babe in the manger is the King of Kings and Lord of Lords! Bow before him in worship!

For Kids and Families: Tell about the favorite Christmas gift you've ever received.

Discuss:
- What's on your Christmas list this year?
- During such an exciting season, how can we make sure we're thinking more about Jesus than about the gifts we'll be receiving?

DECEMBER 22

As Ugly as Sin

Read Luke 22

"Lord, shall we strike with the sword?"
(Luke 22:49)

Christmas—"It's the most wonderful time of the year," a beautiful season adorned with lights and holly, echoing with carols and greetings. Yet as we come to the end of Luke, we are reminded of the *reason* we have Christmas. That reason is, as they say, "as ugly as sin."

Luke shares some ugly things in chapter 22:

- petty jealousy and positioning—in the church!
- friends who cannot stay awake—for even an hour!
- the betrayal of Jesus—with a kiss!

- folding in the face of pressure—by dear friends!
- violence by the powerful—against the innocent!

In the midst of all this ugliness we are confronted by an-other: the instinctive recourse to violence: "Lord, shall we strike with the sword?" Yes, it is understandable because Jesus had told them, "Let the one who has no sword sell his cloak and buy one" (v. 36). But those words were clearly symbolic. Jesus had told them that two swords were enough! Even then, the disciples didn't "get" his obvious sarcasm.

Why? Because their hearts did not *want* to "get" it. They had a *heart condition*—sin. This instinctive ugliness ex-plains the ugly things they did. And this heart condition explains the ugly things *we* do. And that is the reason for Christmas. The angel on a Bethlehem hillside said, "Unto you is born this day in the city of David a Savior" (Luke 2:11). From what shall he save us? "You shall call his name Jesus, for he will save his people from their sins" (Matthew 1:21).

Oh, beautiful, beautiful Savior!

———— ✳ ————

Prayer: Thank you, Lord Jesus, for this beautiful season. You have given us "a beautiful headdress instead of ashes, the oil of gladness instead of mourning, the garment of praise instead of a faint spirit" [Isaiah 61:3]. You are indeed a beautiful Savior! In your precious name we pray. Amen.

Consider: What are some beautiful things happening in the world today?

What are some ugly things taking place? Thank God that Jesus came to transform all this ugliness into beauty.

For Further Study and Reflection: Is "the sword" misused in our society? If so, when? What is the proper use of "the sword"?

Reflect: What do you need to take "the sword" to? What ugliness in your life needs the transforming touch of Jesus?

For Kids and Families: See how fast each member of the family can say the letters of the alphabet. Don't be afraid to get silly with this! Take this opportunity to present the ABCs of salvation to your children:

A = We are all sinners, and we must ADMIT this.

B = We must BELIEVE that Jesus died to save us from our sins.

C = We must CONFESS that Jesus is Lord and offer our lives to him.

Take time together to pray. Allow your children the chance to pray a prayer of salvation if they have not already done so. Even children who have prayed for this before may find comfort in offering themselves to Jesus again.

Discuss:

- How does it make you feel to know that Jesus is your Savior?

DECEMBER 23

Come, Thou Long-Expected Jesus

Read Luke 23

*"When Herod saw Jesus, he was very glad, for he had
long desired to see him."* (Luke 23:8)

In 1744 Charles Wesley was distressed by the condition of the poor and orphans in Great Britain. Longing for the return of the Lord and the restoration of justice, Wesley wrote the Advent hymn "Come, Thou Long-Expected Jesus." His thought was that as we remember Christ's first coming we would be stirred to prepare for his second coming.

Luke wrote of a man who had longed to see Jesus: King Herod. Longing to see Jesus is a good thing usually, but in this instance we need to consider the motivation behind Herod's longing. While Wesley longed for justice, Herod longed to see Jesus work a miracle or otherwise entertain him. He was amused by Jesus, not amazed by him.

When we count the days and anticipate the arrival of Christmas, what are our motives? Is Christmas about being amused or being amazed? The presents or the presence? Plunder or wonder?

Let us approach Christmas with a true desire to see Jesus:

> *Come, Thou long-expected Jesus,*
> *Born to set Thy people free.*
> *From our fears and sins release us;*
> *Let us find our rest in thee.*
> *Israel's Strength and Consolation,*
> *Hope of all the earth Thou art—*
> *Dear Desire of every nation,*
> *Joy of every longing heart!*
>
> *Born Thy people to deliver,*
> *Born a child and yet a King,*
> *Born to reign in us forever,*
> *Now Thy gracious kingdom bring.*
> *By Thine own eternal Spirit,*
> *Rule in all our hearts alone.*
> *By thine all-sufficient merit,*
> *Raise us to Thy glorious throne.*
>
> —Charles Wesley

Prayer: Jesus, forgive me when I long for Christmas for all the wrong reasons. Help me celebrate Christmas with a sincere desire to honor you and help my "neighbor." In your name I pray. Amen.

Consider: How are we amused by Christmas? How can we be amazed?

How can we invite the presence of Jesus more fully into our Christmas celebrations?

For Further Study and Reflection: Research the Dark Ages. Why were they called "dark"? How do they compare to today?

Reflect: As you consider your life, what is the most pressing thing that causes you to pray, "Come, Thou long-expected Jesus"? Will you commit that thing to God?

For Kids and Families: Tell knock-knock jokes together. If you need ideas, there are lists online. Try to see if you can make up some new ones together.

Discuss:
- What makes these silly jokes so amusing?
- How can we make sure we're remembering that Christmas isn't about being amused but rather about being amazed at what God has done?

———— ✳ ————

DECEMBER 24

Can You Hear the Bells on Christmas Eve?

Read Luke 24

"Peace to you!" (Luke 24:36)

I love Christmas Eve, especially singing "Silent Night" as we light candles around the sanctuary. When all candles are lit and the room is filled with soft light, the faces around glow with calm wonder. The Lord is near, and I feel such a peace.

Peace—it can be elusive, can't it? One Christmas carol by Henry Wadsworth Longfellow goes,

> *And in despair I bowed my head.*
> *"There is no peace on earth," I said,*
> *"For hate is strong, and mocks the song*
> *Of peace on earth, good-will to men."*

When Jesus rose from the dead he came to a group of men who were hiding in fear and confusion. The man to whom they had dedicated their lives, the leader they had vowed to follow, the friend who had loved them unconditionally—Jesus—had been executed by the state three days prior. Their dreams had died. Their hopes had been shattered. Their peace had been disturbed. "Jesus himself . . . said to them, 'Peace to you!'" I'm not sure, but it seems that the appearance of a dead man in a room with locked doors would probably cause more anxiety than peace. But this was just who they needed to give them peace.

Perhaps the peace of Christmas has been swallowed up by the hectic pace, by family squabbles, by insecurity or disappointment. Perhaps you are hiding in fear and confusion. Perhaps someone you love is no longer "home for Christmas." There is one who cannot be kept out by death or fear or closed doors. He is with you, right now, in the room where you are hiding. And his word to you is—"Peace."

———— ✳ ————

Prayer: Jesus, thank you for giving peace in times of turmoil. As I consider your birth and your resurrection, help me to have and to share your peace. In your name I pray. Amen.

Consider: In what area of your life do you most need Jesus' peace right now? How can you gain it?

Whom can you help find the peace of Jesus? How will you do it?

For Further Study and Reflection: Do an Internet search for "current wars on earth." Pray for the people who are impacted by war's devastation.

Reflect: Read Hebrews 11:35–40. Pray for Christians who are undergoing persecution. Ask God to give them peace, hope, and protection this Christmas.

For Kids and Families: Sing or listen to "Silent Night" together. If your situation will allow it safely, light some candles while you enjoy the singing.

Discuss:
- What does this song make you think about?
- Why do you think we associate silence with peace?
- In what area of your life do you most need Jesus' peace now?

DECEMBER 25

Merry Christmas!

Read Luke 2:1–20

In those days a decree went out from Caesar Augustus that all the world should be registered. This was the first registration when Quirinius was governor of Syria. And all went to be registered, each to his own town. And Joseph also went up from Galilee, from the town of Nazareth, to Judea, to the city of David, which is called Bethlehem, because he was of the house and lineage of David, to be registered with Mary, his betrothed, who was with child. And while they were there, the time came for her to give birth. And she gave birth to her firstborn son and wrapped him in swaddling cloths and laid him in a manger, because there was no place for them in the inn.

And in the same region there were shepherds out in the field, keeping watch over their flock by night. And an angel of the Lord appeared to them, and the glory of the Lord shone around them, and they were filled with great fear. And the angel said to them, "Fear not, for behold, I bring you good news of great joy that will be for all the people. For unto you is born this day in the city of David a Savior, who is Christ the Lord. And this will be a sign for you: you will find a baby wrapped in swaddling cloths and lying in a manger."

And suddenly there was with the angel a multitude of the heavenly host praising God and saying, "Glory to God in the highest, and on earth peace among those with whom he is pleased!"

When the angels went away from them into heaven, the shepherds said to one another, "Let us go over to Bethlehem and see this thing that has happened, which the Lord has made known to us." And they went with haste and found Mary and Joseph, and the baby lying in a manger. And when they saw it, they made known the saying that had been told them concerning this child.

And all who heard it wondered at what the shepherds told them. But Mary treasured up all these things, pondering them in her heart. And the shepherds returned, glorifying and praising God for all they had heard and seen, as it had been told them.

---　✳　---

Prayer:

> *Thank you, Lord Jesus, on this*
> *Christmas morn,*
> *That you came to humble earth to be born.*
> *In stable low, in cattle stall,*
> *You came that day to save us all.*
> *May we, this day, each do our part,*
> *By asking you to come into our heart.*
> *Amen.*

—Scott Wade

For Everyone: After reading the Christmas story together, talk about the importance of this story. Discuss ways you can keep the spirit of Christmas alive beyond this day.

OTHER BOOKS BY SCOTT WADE

THE CLIMB
A five-year devotional guide through the Bible

BOOK 1: *START HERE*
New Testament, Psalms, and Genesis—Numbers

BOOK 2: *STAY FOCUSED*
New Testament, Psalms, and Deuteronomy—1 Kings

BOOK 3: *STICK WITH IT*
New Testament, Psalms, and 2 Kings—Job

BOOK 4: *STRETCH YOURSELF*
New Testament, Psalms, Proverbs, Isaiah, and Jeremiah

BOOK 5: *STAND TALL*
New Testament, Psalms, Ecclesiastes, Song of Solomon,
and Lamentations—Malachi

• •

How to order:
Visit the Momentum Ministries website at
www.momentumministries.org
to order copies of this and other books to help you attain,
maintain, and regain spiritual momentum.

ABOUT THE AUTHORS

Scott Wade and his wife, Lana, *love* Christmas! Scott's favorite preparation for Christmas is cutting down a huge Christmas tree and decorating it along with the rest of the house and yard. For Lana it has to be cooking and preparing for the arrival of children and grandchildren—and getting the choir ready for the Christmas musicals she has led for many years. The Wades have three daughters along with their husbands and seven grandchildren. Scott and Lana served together in pastoral ministry for twenty-nine years before feeling called by the Lord to "get out of the boat" and begin a new thing: Momentum Ministries. With an emphasis on writing and preaching, Pastor Scott seeks to help individuals and churches attain, maintain, and regain spiritual momentum. Scott and Lana now reside on Johns Island, South Carolina.

Matt and Fay Wagner contributed the activities and questions for the devotional sections titled "For Kids and Families." The Wagners are public school educators near Cincinnati, Ohio. They believe God has called them to this area of service. When not at school they like to travel and have led several mission trips. Their favorite Christmas tradition is baking cookies and decorating them with their family. They enjoy their holidays with their daughter, Hillary; son, Robert; and "daughter-in-love," Aimee.